W9-BYM-079

HOUGHTON MIFFLIN
Reading
A Legacy of Literacy

Family and Friends

HOUGHTON MIFFLIN   BOSTON • MORRIS PLAINS, NJ

California • Colorado • Georgia • Illinois • New Jersey • Texas

Printed in the U.S.A.

ISBN 0-618-16200-3

3456789-BS-06 05 04 03 02

Design, Art Management, and Page Production: Studio Goodwin Sturges

Contents

Hot Dog

by Lorraine Merrill
illustrated by Renée Andriani

Floss has a dog called Hot Dog.

Hot Dog can do flips.

Hot Dog can flop on top.

Floss is glad to have Hot Dog.

Tom's Plan

by Rafael Lopez
illustrated by Enzo Giannini

Tom gets a big black pen.
Tom plans his family picture.

Here is Tom and
his pet dog, Cliff.

On top, Tom adds Dad.
Tom adds Mom.

Tom gets lots of love from
Cliff, Mom, and Dad.

Jock's Hut

by Denise Zimmer

illustrated by Alexi Natchev

Jock gets big flags,
glass clocks, and brass
jugs in his hut.

Jock gets blocks, cribs,
and socks in his hut.

Moms, dads, and children
look in Jock's hut.

People love Jock's hut!

Knock, Knock

by Sid Jones
illustrated by Miki Yamamoto

Knock, knock!
Who is it?

Ken.

Ken who?

Ken you stop knock, knocking?

Press the tin bell quick!

Knock, knock.
Who is it?

Skip.

Skip who?

Skip the tin bell. Step on in.

Miss Nell

by Ruth Kwan
illustrated by Betina Ogden

Nell said, "Let's play, Stan.
I am Miss Nell."

"Let's read, Stan.

Let's write, Stan," said Miss Nell.

"Spell *bed*, *tell*, *rest*, Stan,"
Miss Nell said.

"Let's skip fast, Stan.
Let's skip, skip, skip!"

Deb and Bess

by Virginia Houston
illustrated by Melissa Sweet

Deb's best friend is Bess.
Knock, knock, knock!

"Let's plan today, Bess,"
said Deb.
"Let's swim fast, Deb,"
said Bess.

Bess got wet.

She swims fast, fast, fast.

Deb swims fast, fast, fast, too!

Buzzing Bug

by Shiyun Wong
illustrated by Paul Hayes

One black bug can buzz in the hot sun.
Buzz, buzz, buzz!

One black bug can spin a
big web.
Spin, spin, spin!

Splat!
One bug is stuck.

Can the bug get away?

Duff in the Mud

by Wayne Mazzola

illustrated by Susan Kathleen Hartung

Duff can walk in the mud.
Splat!

Gus must scrub Duff
in their big red tub.

Gus will not hurt Duff.

Duff will not fuss in the tub.

Jess and Mom

by Diane Patek
illustrated by K. D. Maxx

Mom's red car has rust.

Jess and Mom must get
on the big tan bus.

Jess can hear gulls on the strip.
The gulls strut, strut, strut.

Ten gulls get scraps from Jess.
Ten gulls strut, strut, strut.

Word Lists

Hot Dog **(p. 5)** accompanies *Who's in a Family?*

DECODABLE WORDS

Target Skills
Consonant Clusters with *l:*
flips, flop, Floss, glad

Short *o:*
Dog, flop, Floss, Hot, top

Words Using Previously Taught Skills
can, has

HIGH-FREQUENCY WORDS

Previously Taught
a, called, do, have, is, on, to

Tom's Plan **(p. 9)** accompanies *Who's in a Family?*

DECODABLE WORDS

Target Skills
Consonant Clusters with *l:*
black, Cliff, plan, plans

Short *o:*
dog, from, lots, Mom, Tom, Tom's, top

Words Using Previously Taught Skills
adds, big, Dad, gets, his, pen, pet,

HIGH-FREQUENCY WORDS

New
family, love, picture

Previously Taught
a, and, here, is, on, of

Theme 4, Week 1
Jock's Hut (p. 13) accompanies *Who's in a Family?*

DECODABLE WORDS

Target Skills
Consonant Clusters with *l*:
blocks, clocks, flags, glass

Short *o*:
blocks, clocks, Jock, Jock's, moms, socks

Words Using Previously Taught Skills
big, brass, cribs, dads, gets, his, hut, jugs

HIGH-FREQUENCY WORDS

New
children, love, people

Previously Taught
and, in, look

Theme 4, Week 2
Knock, Knock (p. 17) accompanies *The Best Pet.*

DECODABLE WORDS

Target Skills
Consonant Clusters with *s*:
Skip, step, stop

Short *e*:
bell, Ken, press, step

Silent *kn*:
knock, knocking

Words Using Previously Taught Skills
it, quick, tin

HIGH-FREQUENCY WORDS

Previously Taught
in, is, on, the, who, you

Miss Nell (p. 21) accompanies *The Best Pet.*

DECODABLE WORDS

Target Skills
Consonant Clusters with *s*:
fast, rest, skip, spell, Stan

Short *e*:
bed, let's, Nell, rest, spell, tell

Words Using Previously Taught Skills
am, Miss

HIGH-FREQUENCY WORDS

New
play, read, write

Previously Taught
I, said

Deb and Bess (p. 25) accompanies *The Best Pet.*

DECODABLE WORDS

Target Skills
Consonant Clusters with *s*:
best, fast, swim, swims

Short *e*:
Bess, best, Deb, Deb's, let's, wet

Silent *kn*:
knock

Words Using Previously Taught Skills
got, plan

HIGH-FREQUENCY WORDS

New
friend, she, today

Previously Taught
is, said, too

Theme 4, Week 3
Buzzing Bug **(p. 29)** accompanies *Bud's Day Out.*

DECODABLE WORDS

Target Skills
Triple Clusters:
splat

Short *u*:
bug, buzz, buzzing, stuck, sun

Words Using Previously Taught Skills
big, black, can, get, hot, spin, web

HIGH-FREQUENCY WORDS

Previously Taught
a, away, in, is, one, the

Theme 4, Week 3
Duff in the Mud **(p. 33)** accompanies *Bud's Day Out.*

DECODABLE WORDS

Target Skills
Triple Clusters:
scrub, splat

Short *u*:
Duff, fuss, Gus, mud, must, scrub, tub

Words Using Previously Taught Skills
big, can, red, will

HIGH-FREQUENCY WORDS

New
hurt, their, walk

Previously Taught
in, not, the

Jess and Mom (p. 37) accompanies *Bud's Day Out.*

DECODABLE WORDS

Target Skills
Triple Clusters:
scraps, strip, strut

Short *u:*
bus, gulls, must, rust, strut

Words Using Previously Taught Skills
big, can, from, get, has, Jess, Mom, Mom's, red, tan, ten

HIGH-FREQUENCY WORDS

New
car, hear

Previously Taught
and, on, the

HIGH-FREQUENCY WORDS TAUGHT TO DATE

a	color	for	I	never	shall	we
all	come	four	in	not	she	what
also	do	friend	is	of	sing	where
and	does	full	jump	on	some	who
animal	down	funny	know	once	the	why
are	eat	girl	learn	one	their	would
away	every	go	like	paper	they	write
bird	fall	green	live	people	three	you
blue	family	have	look	picture	to	your
brown	father	he	love	play	today	
call	find	hear	many	pull	too	
car	first	here	me	read	two	
children	five	hold	mother	said	upon	
cold	flower	hurt	my	see	walk	

Decoding skills taught to date: Consonants *m, s, t, c,* consonants *n, f, p,* short *a,* consonants *b, r, h, g,* short *i,* consonants *d, w, l, x,* short *o,* consonants *y, k, v,* short *e,* consonants *q, j, z,* short *u,* double final consonants, final consonants, plurals with *-s,* verb endings *-s, -ed, -ing,* possessives, consonant clusters with *r,* contractions with *-'s,* clusters with *l,* clusters with *s,* silent consonants *kn, wr, gn,* triple clusters